This Journal Belongs To:

_____

_____

_____

I guide you in the way of wisdom and lead you along straight paths.

Proverbs 4:11
(NIV)

Enjoy serving the LORD, and he will give you what you want.

Psalm 37:4
(NCV)

*Draw near
to God and
he will draw
near to you.*

James 4:8 (NIV)

And he himself has promised us this: eternal life.

1 John 2:25

(TLB)

For great is the LORD, and greatly to be praised: he also is to be feared above all gods.

1 Chronicles 16:25 (KJV)

He will yet fill your mouth with laughter and your lips with shouts of joy.

Job 8:21 (NIV)

The eternal God is your refuge, and underneath are the everlasting arms.

Deuteronomy 33:27 *(TLB)*

Training your body helps you in some ways, but serving God helps you in every way by bringing you blessings in this life and in the future life, too.

1 Timothy 4:8 (NCV)

*Let us not
become weary in
doing good, for
at the proper
time we will reap
a harvest if we
do not give up.*

Galatians 6:9 (NIV)

As a mother comforts her child, so will I comfort you.

Isaiah 66:13
(NIV)

*Our soul
waits for the
LORD; he is
our help and
our shield.*

Psalm 33:20
(NASB)

The fear of the LORD is the beginning of wisdom and the knowledge of the Holy One is understanding.

Proverbs 9:10 (NASB)

And we know that in all things God works for the good of those who love him, who have been called according to his purpose.

Romans 8:28 (NIV)

Good news makes you feel better. Your happiness will show in your eyes.

Proverbs 15:30
(NCV)

I will say
of the LORD,
"He is my
refuge and my
fortress, my
God, in him
will I trust."

Psalm 91:2 (KJV)

Your word is a lamp to my feet and a light for my path.

Psalm 119:105
(NIV)

May the LORD
bring you into an
ever deeper under-
standing of the
love of God and of
the patience that
comes from Christ.

2 Thessalonians 3:5
(TLB)

The Father himself loves you. He loves you because you loved me and believed that I came from God.

John 16:27 (NCV)

The LORD will give strength to His people; The LORD will bless His people with peace.

Psalm 29:11
(NASB)

In his heart a man plans his course, but the LORD determines his steps.

Proverbs 16:9 (NIV)

Don't worry about anything; instead, pray about every-thing; tell God your needs and don't forget to thank him for his answers.

Philippians 4:6 (TLB)

"*For I know the plans I have for you*," declares the LORD, "*plans to prosper you and not to harm you, plans to give you hope and a future.*"

Jeremiah 29:11 (NIV)

The LORD
will guard
you as you
come and go,
both now
and forever.

Psalm 121:8 (NCV)

I will not forget you. Behold, I have inscribed you on the palms of My hands.

Isaiah 49:15–16
(NASB)

The LORD will fight for you; you need only to be still.

Exodus 14:14 (NIV)

There is none holy as the LORD: for there is none beside thee: neither is there any rock like our God.

1 Samuel 2:2 (KJV)

This is the day that the LORD has made. Let us rejoice and be glad today!

Psalm 118: 24 (NCV)

He will yet fill your mouth with laughter and your lips with shouts of joy.

Job 8:21 (NIV)

I love all
who love me.
Those who
search for me
shall surely
find me.

Proverbs 8:17

(TLB)

You know the LORD *is full of mercy and is kind.*

James 5:11
(NCV)

Cast your burden upon the LORD, and He will sustain you; He will never allow the righteous to be shaken.

Psalm 55:22 (NASB)

I will rejoice greatly in the LORD, My soul will exult in my God; For He has clothed me with garments of sal-vation, He has wrapped me with a robe of righteousness.

Isaiah 61:10 (NASB)

For the LORD gives wisdom, and from his mouth come knowledge and understanding. He holds victory in store for the upright.

Proverbs 2:6 (NIV)

The LORD your God is with you, he is mighty to save. He will take great delight in you, he will quiet you with his love, he will rejoice over you with singing.

Zephaniah 3:17 (NIV)

It is God himself
who has made us
what we are and
given us new lives
from Christ Jesus;
and long ages ago
he planned that
we should spend
these lives in
helping others.

Ephesians 2:10 (TLB)

Trust in the LORD with all your heart and lean not on your own understanding; in all your ways acknowledge him and he will make your paths straight.

Proverbs 3:5–6 (NIV)

*Depend on
the LORD
in whatever
you do, and
your plans
will succeed.*

Proverbs 16:3
(NCV)

God demonstrates His own love toward us, in that while we were yet sinners, Christ died for us.

Romans 5:8
(NASB)

For this God is our God for ever and ever: he will be our guide even unto death.

Psalm 48:14
(KJV)

Submit yourselves therefore to God. Resist the devil, and he will flee from you. Draw nigh to God, and he will draw nigh to you.

James 4:7–8 (KJV)

For God so loved the world that he gave his one and only Son, that whoever believes in him shall not perish but have everlasting life.

John 3:16 (NIV)

Do you not know? Have you not heard? The LORD is the everlasting God, the Creator of the ends of the earth. He will not grow tired or weary, and his understanding no one can fathom.

Isaiah 40:28 (NIV)

*Every word
of God
proves true.
He defends
all who come
to him for
protection.*

Proverbs 30:5
(TLB)

Since we have a Kingdom nothing can destroy, let us please God by serving him with thankful hearts, and with holy fear and awe.

Hebrews 12:28 *(TLB)*

Let the words of my mouth, and the meditation of my heart, be acceptable in thy sight, O LORD, my strength, and my redeemer.

Psalm 19:14 (KJV)

Praise the Lord All-Powerful, because the Lord is good! His love continues forever.

Jeremiah 33:11
(NCV)

*Fear God
and obey his
command-
ments, for
this is the
entire duty
of man.*

Ecclesiastes 12:13
(TLB)

*Hope
deferred
makes the
heart sick,
but desire
fulfilled is a
tree of life.*

Proverbs 13:12
(NASB)

_If_ you confess
with your mouth,
"Jesus is LORD,"
and believe in
your heart that
God raised him
from the dead,
you will be saved.

Romans 10:9
(NIV)

But if we walk in the light, as he is in the light, we have fellowship one with another, and the blood of Jesus Christ his Son cleanseth us from all sin.

1 John 1:7 (KJV)

The LORD is close to those whose hearts are breaking; he rescues those who are humbly sorry for their sins.

Psalms 34:18
(TLB)

*If any of you
lacks wisdom,
let him ask of
God, who gives
to all men
generously
and without
reproach, and
it will be given
to him.*

James 1:5 (NASB)

For thou art my rock and my fortress; therefore for thy name's sake lead me, and guide me.

Psalm 31:3 *(KJV)*

He is beloved of God and lives in safety beside Him. God surrounds him with his loving care, and preserves him from every harm.

Deuteronomy 33:12 *(TLB)*

The LORD is my helper, I will not be afraid.

Hebrews 13:6 (NASB)

My God will meet all your needs according to his glorious riches in Christ Jesus.

Philippians 4:19
(NIV)

God is our refuge and strength, a very present help in trouble.

Psalm 46:1 (KJV)

The wicked man flees though no one pursues, but the righteous are as bold as a lion.

Proverbs 8:1 (NIV)

Show me your ways, O LORD, teach me your paths; guide me, for you are God my Savior, and my hope is in you all day long.

Psalm 25:4–5 (NIV)

The LORD's loved ones will lie down in safety, because he protects them all day long. The ones he loves rest with him.

Deuteronomy 33:12
(NCV)

For your kingdom never ends. You rule generation after generation.

Psalm 145:13
(TLB)

And walk in love, as Christ also hath loved us, and hath given himself for us an offering and a sacrifice to God for a sweet-smelling savour.

Ephesians 5:2 (KJV)

The LORD
sustains all
who fall,
And raises
up all who
are bowed
down.

Psalm 145:14
(NASB)

Do not be afraid. I bring you good news of great joy that will be for all the people.

Luke 2:10 (NIV)

Now faith is
the substance
of things
hoped for, the
evidence of
things
not seen.

Hebrews 11:1 (KJV)

The LORD All-Powerful is with us; the God of Jacob is our defender.

Psalm 46:7 (NCV)

But those who hope in the LORD will renew their strength. They will soar on wings like eagles; they will run and not grow weary, they will walk and not be faint.

Isaiah 40:31 (NIV)

Blessed be Jehovah God, the God of Israel, who only does wonderful things.

Psalm 72:18 (TLB)

*I can do
all things
through
Him who
strengthens
me.*

Philippians
4:13 (NASB)

This is what real love is: It is not our love for God; it is God's love for us in sending his Son to be the way to take away our sins.

1 John 4:10 (NCV)

Great peace have they which love thy law: and nothing shall offend them.

Psalm 119:165
(KJV)

Like apples of gold in settings of silver is a word spoken in right circumstances.

Proverbs 25:11 *(NASB)*

The prayer of a right-eous man is powerful and effective.

James 5:10 (NIV)

Praise the LORD, God our Savior, who helps us every day.

Psalm 68:19 (NCV)

A relaxed
attitude
lengthens a
man's life;
jealousy rots
it away

Proverbs 14:30
(TLB)

Don't be sad, because the joy of the LORD will make you strong.

Nehemiah 8:10
(NCV)

If any of you lacks wisdom, he should ask God, who gives generously to all without finding fault, and it will be given to him.

James 1:5 (NIV)

Let us hold firmly to the hope that we have confessed, because we can trust God to do what he promised.

Hebrews 10:23 (NCV)

You will
seek Me and
find Me when
you search for
Me with all
your heart.

Jeremiah 29:13
(NASB)

But if we walk in the light, as he is in the light, we have fellowship with one another, and the blood of Jesus, his Son, purifies us of all sin.

1 John 1:7 (NIV)

Those who trust in the Lord are steady like Mount Zion, unmoved by any circumstance.

Psalm 125:1 (TLB)

I am not ashamed: for I know whom I have believed, and am persuaded that he is able to keep that which I have committed unto him against that day.

2 Timothy 1:12 (KJV)

The Son of Man came to find lost people and save them.

Luke 19:10 (NCV)

The LORD is my rock and my fortress and my deliverer. My God, my rock, in whom I take refuge.

Psalm 18:2 (NASB)

For the eyes of the LORD are intently watching all who live good lives, and he gives attention when they cry to him.

Psalm 34:15 (TLB)

My soul finds rest in God alone; my salvation comes from him.

Psalm 62:1
(NIV)

Do not be
deceived: Bad
company corrupts
good morals.

1 Corinthians 15:33
(NASB)

He will swallow up death in victory; and the LORD GOD will wipe away tears from off all faces.

Isaiah 25:8 (KJV)

He who sows
righteousness
reaps a sure
reward.

Proverbs 11:18
(KJV)

The world and its desires pass away, but the man who does the will of God lives forever.

1 John 2:17 (NIV)

Then you will call, and the Lord will answer; you will cry for help, and he will say: Here am I.

Isaiah 58:9 (NIV)

For
where your
treasure is,
there will
your heart
be also.

Luke 12:34
(NASB)

He will shield you with his wings! They will shelter you. His faithful promises are your armor.

Psalm 91:4 (TLB)

Ask and it shall be given to you; seek and ye shall find; knock and it shall be opened unto you.

Matthew 7:7 (KJV)

I tell you the truth, anything truth, anything you did for even the least of my people here, you also did for me.

Matthew 25:40 (NCV)

Cast all your anxiety upon Him, because He cares for you.

1 Peter 5:7 (NASB)

There is salvation in no one else! Under all heaven there is no other name for men to call upon to save them.

Acts 4:12 (TLB)

There is therefore now no condemnation to them which are in Christ Jesus.

Romans 8:1 (KJV)

Go and make followers
of all people in the
world. Baptize them in
the name of the Father
and the Son and the
Holy Spirit. Teach them
to obey everything that I
have taught you, and I
will be with you always.

Matthew 28:19–20 (NCV)

The Lord will reign forever, Thy God, O Zion, to all generations. Praise the Lord!

Psalm 146:10
(NASB)

*In the begin-
ning there was
the Word. The
Word was with
God, and the
Word was God.*

John 1:1 (NCV)

Never tire of loyalty and kindness. Hold these virtues tightly. Write them deep within your heart.

Proverbs 3:3 (TLB)

Let everything that has breath praise the Lord. Praise the Lord!

Psalm 150:1
(NASB)

When people insult you because you follow Christ, you are blessed, because the glorious Spirit, the Spirit of God, is with you.

1 Peter 4:14 (NCV)

The fear of the LORD is the beginning of knowledge; fools despise wisdom and instruction.

Proverbs 1:7 (NASB)

Know that the LORD is God. He made us, and we belong to him; we are his people, the sheep he tends.

Psalm 100:3 (NCV)

Be full of love for
others, following the
example of Christ
who loved you and
gave himself to God
as a sacrifice to take
away your sins.

Ephesians 5:2 *(TLB)*

The LORD
hath done
great things
for us; whereof
we are glad.

Psalm 26:3 *(KJV)*

Live in the fear of the Lord always.

Proverbs 23:17

(NASB)

I have given them the glory you gave me— the glorious unity of being one, as we are.

John 17:22 (TLB)

Punishment that hurts chases evil from the heart.

Proverbs 20:30
(TLB)

Every man's way is right in his own eyes. But the LORD weighs the hearts.

Proverbs 21:2 (NASB)

I will be a Father to you, and you will be my sons and daughters, says the Almighty.

2 Corinthians 6:18 (NIV)

Jesus lives forever and continues to be a Priest so that no one else is needed.

Hebrews 7:24

(TLB)

I will praise
the name of
God with a
song, and
will magnify
him with
thanksgiving.

Psalm 69:30 (KJV)

For where two or three are gathered together in my name, there am I in the midst of them.

Matthew 18:20 (KJV)

There is a time for everything, and a season for every activity under heaven.

Ecclesiastes 3:1
(NIV)

Seek the LORD and his strength, seek his face continually.

1 Chronicles
16:11 (KJV)

*Be careful—
watch out for
attacks from
Satan, your
great enemy.
He prowls
around like a
hungry, roaring
lion, looking for
some victim to
tear apart.*

1 Peter 5:1 (TLB)

You must return to your God, maintain love and justice, and wait for your God always.

Hosea 12:6 (NIV)

Doing what is right and fair is more important to the LORD than sacrifices.

Proverbs 21:3 (NCV)

For the wages of sin is death, but the gift of God is eternal life in Christ Jesus our Lord.

Romans 6:23 (NIV)

But as many as received him, to them gave he power to become the sons of God, even to them that believe on his name.

John 1:12 (KJV)

But seek ye first the kingdom of God, and his righteousness; and all these things shall be added unto you.

Matthew 6:33 (KJV)

Now may the Lord of peace give you peace at all times and in every way. The Lord be with all of you.

2 Thessalonians 3:16 (NCV)

When you lie down, you will not be afraid; when you lie down your sleep will be sweet.

Proverbs 3:24 (NASB)